A Note to Parents

DK READERS is a compelling programme for beginning readers, designed in conjunction with leading literacy experts, including Dr. Linda Gambrell, Distinguished Professor of Education at Clemson University. Dr. Gambrell has served as President of the National Reading Conference, the College Reading Association, and the International Reading Association.

Beautiful illustrations and superb full-colour photographs combine with engaging, easy-to-read stories to offer a fresh approach to each subject in the series. Each DK READER is guaranteed to capture a child's interest while developing his or her reading skills, general knowledge, and love of reading.

The five levels of DK READERS are aimed at different reading abilities, enabling you to choose the books that are exactly right for your child:

Pre-level 1: Learning to read
Level 1: Beginning to read
Level 2: Beginning to read alone
Level 3: Reading alone
Level 4: Proficient readers

The "normal" age at which a child begins to read can be anywhere from three to eight years old. Adult participation through the lower levels is very helpful for providing encouragement, discussing storylines, and sounding out unfamiliar words.

No matter which level you select, you can be sure that you are helping your child learn to read, then read to learn!

LONDON, NEW YORK, MUNICH,
MELBOURNE, and DELHI

For DK/BradyGames

Title Manager Tim Fitzpatrick
Cover Designer Tim Amrhein
Production Designer Tracy Wehmeyer
Vice President & Publisher Mike Degler
Editor-In-Chief H. Leigh Davis
Licensing Manager Christian Sumner
Marketing Manager Katie Hemlock
Digital Publishing Manager Tim Cox
Operations Manager Stacey Beheler
Reading Consultant Linda B. Gambrell, Ph.D.
Anglicisation Scarlett O'Hara

For WWE

Global Publishing Manager Steve Pantaleo
Photo Department Frank Vitucci,
Josh Tottenham, Jamie Nelson, Mike Moran,
JD Sestito, Melissa Halladay, Lea Girard
Legal Lauren Dienes-Middlen

First published in Great Britain in 2014 by
Dorling Kindersley Limited
80 Strand, London, WC2R 0RL

10 9 8 7 6 5 4 3 2 1
001–259388–June/14

Page design copyright © 2014 Dorling Kindersley Limited

A CIP catalogue record for this book is available
from the British Library.

ISBN: 978-0-24100-745-7

Colour reproduction in the UK by Altaimage
Printed and bound in China

The publisher would like to thank the following for their kind
permission to reproduce their photographs:
All photos courtesy WWE Entertainment, Inc.

All other images © Dorling Kindersley
For further information see: www.dkimages.com

Discover more at
www.dk.com

CM Punk®

SECOND EDITION

Written by Kevin Sullivan

CM Punk is one of the most popular Superstars in WWE. Fans from all over the world cheer his name every time he steps into the ring. He is also one of the most successful Superstars ever. In fact, the rebellious Punk held the WWE Championship longer than any other Superstar since Hulk Hogan, who was champion in the 1980s.

CM Punk likes to think he's the "Best in the World". Looking at his achievements, it's hard to dispute his claim.

However, Punk wasn't always one of WWE's greatest stars. He was once just a youngster trying his best to get into WWE. His journey was long, but thanks to his hard work, he accomplished his dreams.

Punk's journey began in his hometown of Chicago, USA, where he was one of four children. As a boy, he liked to watch WWE on television. He dreamed of following in the footsteps of his heroes "Rowdy" Roddy Piper and Jimmy "Superfly" Snuka.

As he grew older, Punk saw people around him drinking too much and taking drugs. Instead of doing the same thing, he spent his time listening to punk music.

Like a lot of fans of punk music, CM Punk made a promise to himself to live a "straight edge" life. That meant that he would not get into trouble by taking drugs or drinking too much. Instead, he worked hard at his goal of one day becoming WWE Champion.

Punk began training to become a professional wrestler under Ace Steel at a wrestling school in the Midwestern states of the USA. Using the skills he learned from Steel, he spent the next few years competing in smaller arenas across the USA.

CM Punk Facts

- CM Punk appeared at *WrestleMania 22* as one of the gangsters who accompanied John Cena to the ring.

- CM Punk's signature diving elbow drop is a tribute to the great Randy Savage.

- CM Punk's arm is tattooed with good luck charms, but he believes you make your own luck through hard work.

- CM Punk is a fan of the Chicago Blackhawks and Chicago Cubs.

CM Punk Stats

Height: 1.88 m
Weight: 99 kg
From: Chicago, USA
Signature Moves:
G.T.S. (Go to Sleep),
Anaconda Vise

All the time, Punk dreamed of becoming a Superstar. In 2005, Punk's hard work finally paid off when he was signed up to a developmental deal by WWE.

Punk made his WWE debut on 4th July 2006, beating Stevie Richards on the ECW show. Over the next few months, the tattooed Superstar beat every ECW competitor he faced, including Mike Knox, Justin Credible, and C.W. Anderson. With each passing victory, Punk gained more and more fans.

His popularity eventually led him to a place in the *Survivor Series* event with Triple H, Shawn Michaels, and The Hardys.

In December, Punk earned an opportunity to compete for the ECW Championship inside an Elimination Chamber. However, he failed to win after being the first Superstar eliminated.

Shortly after the Elimination Chamber Match, Punk lost his first singles match to Hardcore Holly, followed by another loss to Matt Striker. Soon there were rumours that several important people in WWE management didn't think Punk had the skills to be a top star.

Rather than be downcast, Punk remembered his childhood dream of becoming a WWE Champion. That made him work even harder at becoming the "Best in the World."

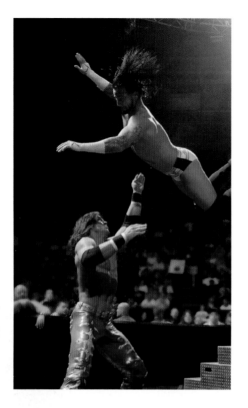

Punk refused to give up. His hard work was rewarded in September 2007, when he beat John Morrison and won the ECW Championship. He held the title for more than four months.

Punk's biggest chance came at *WrestleMania XXIV*, where he won the Money in the Bank Ladder Match.

The win gave Punk the chance to compete for a World Championship whenever he wanted. He wisely chose to wait for the right moment. Then, three months later, he decided to make his move.

With World Heavyweight Champion Edge laid out by the mighty Batista, Punk sprinted from the changing room and demanded his match. It took only a few seconds for Punk to beat Edge. CM Punk was the World Heavyweight Champion.

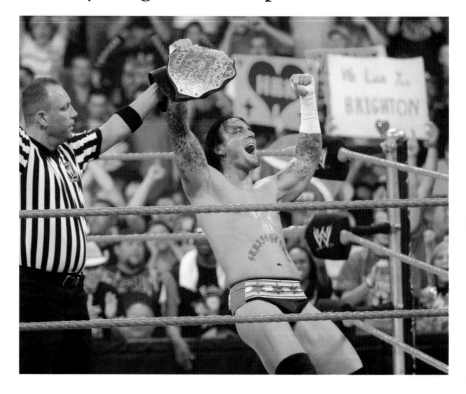

CM Punk Career Highlights

- WWE Champion
- World Heavyweight Champion
- ECW Champion
- World Tag Team Champion
- Intercontinental Champion
- Money in the Bank Ladder Match winner

During his three months as World Heavyweight Champion, Punk beat many bigger opponents, such as Kane and JBL. Many people thought he would have a long reign. However, he was brutally attacked backstage at *Unforgiven* 2008, and was forced to give up his title.

Punk wasn't without gold for long. At *WrestleMania 25*, he once again won the Money in the Bank Ladder Match. Like the year before, the win allowed Punk to compete in a title match whenever he wanted.

This time, he waited until after Jeff Hardy had won the championship in a gruelling Ladder Match at *Extreme Rules.*

Moments later, Punk demanded his match, and once again won the World Heavyweight Championship.

In addition to being a great champion, CM Punk is also one of the best leaders in WWE history. Over his career, he has used his intelligence to convince others to follow him.

First he preached about the importance of a drug-free lifestyle as the head of the Straight Edge Society. Later, he became the leader of the powerful New Nexus.

Straight Edge Society Members

- CM Punk (leader)
- Luke Gallows
- Joseph Mercury
- Serena

New Nexus Members

- CM Punk (leader)
- David Otunga
- Husky Harris
- Michael McGillicutty
- Mason Ryan

In the summer of 2011, CM Punk made his now-famous verbal attack on WWE.  He scolded Vince McMahon, Stephanie McMahon, and Triple H for not running the business of WWE to his liking.

He then threatened to leave WWE completely, but not before claiming he would beat John Cena for the WWE Championship at *Money in the Bank.*

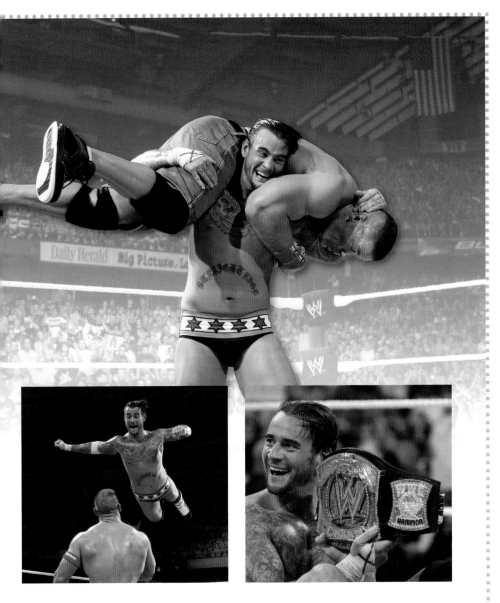

As promised, Punk beat Cena for
the title and left WWE. It was
one of the most shocking events
in WWE history.

In Punk's absence, WWE crowned a new champion. However, "The Second City Saint" would soon return to WWE. Within months, he regained the championship when he beat Alberto Del Rio at *Survivor Series* 2011.

Punk went on to hold the WWE Championship longer than any other Superstar in the modern era.

During his 434 days as champion, he beat some of the greatest competitors in WWE history, including Chris Jericho, Kane, and Big Show. He also aligned himself with Paul Heyman, much to the fans' disappointment.

Punk's epic title reign finally came to an end at *Royal Rumble* 2013, when he lost the gold to The Rock. A few months later he tried to end Undertaker's amazing *WrestleMania* undefeated streak, but he was unable to beat the Phenom.

Following these losses, Punk told Heyman, who he had worked with for a long time, that he no longer wanted him at the ringside for his matches. This angered Heyman, who eventually turned his back on Punk. These events led to

one of the most personal rivalries in WWE history.

Another "Paul Heyman guy" Brock Lesnar beat CM Punk at *SummerSlam* 2013.

Lesnar's win gave Heyman great satisfaction. However, Punk refused to let the loss keep him down. A determined Punk later beat Heyman's two other "guys", Curtis Axel and Ryback, before finally getting his hands on Heyman.

The "Second City Saint" gave his former friend a G.T.S. atop an unforgiving steel cell.

CM Punk never gave up when he was down. Because of his determination, he achieved his lifelong dream of becoming WWE Champion and the "Best in the World".